M000166110

EDITED BY HELEN EXLEY

Published in 2019 by Helen Exley®LONDON in Great Britain.
Illustration by Juliette Clarke © Helen Exley Creative Ltd 2019.
All the words by Pamela Dugdale, Harry Altdon,
Odile Dormeuil, Dalton Exley, Pam Brown, Charlotte Gray,
Helen Thomson, Hannah C. Klein, Helen Exley and
Stuart & Linda Macfarlane © Helen Exley Creative Ltd 2019.
Design, selection and arrangement © Helen Exley Creative Ltd 2019.
The moral right of the author has been asserted.

ISBN 978-1-78485-201-6

12 11 10 9 8 7 6 5 4 3 2 1

OTHER BOOKS IN THE SERIES

THE LITTLE BOOK OF *Gratitude*
THE LITTLE BOOK OF *Happiness*
THE LITTLE BOOK OF *Hope*
THE LITTLE BOOK OF *Smiles*

Helen Exley®LONDON
16 Chalk Hill, Watford, Herts WD19 4BG, UK
www.helenexley.com

THE LITTLE BOOK OF

Kindness

Helen Exley

Kindness is the language which the deaf can hear and blind can see.

MARK TWAIN

Kindness in words
creates confidence,
Kindness in thinking
creates profoundness,
Kindness in giving
creates love.

LAO TZU

Kindness is the golden chain
by which society is bound together.

JOHANN WOLFGANG VON GOETHE

Compassionate action
eradicates poverty, competition,
and violence from our world.

A. T. ARIYARATNE

...a kind word,
a vote of
support is a
charitable gift.

MAYA ANGELOU

Kindness is awesome. It makes our world go round.

HELEN EXLEY

A kind word to one in trouble is often like a switch in a railroad track... an inch between wreck and smooth sailing.

HENRY WARD BEECHER

Be kind; everyone you meet is fighting a hard battle.

JOHN WHITTAKER WATSON

When a man is down, help him up.
When you pass a stranger in the street,
share a smile.
When a person is in need, lend a helping hand.

MUHAMMAD ALI

The centre of human nature
is rooted in ten thousand ordinary acts
of kindness that define our days.

STEPHEN JAY GOULD

Your kindness will spread so quickly,
you couldn't stop it even if you tried!

SIÂN E. MORGAN

Some days the best of kindness
is a simple note, a short email.

HARRY ALTDON

Her little girl was late
arriving home from school
so the mother began to scold her
daughter, but stopped and asked,
"Why are you so late?"
"I had to help another girl.
She was in trouble,"
replied the daughter.
"What did you do to help her?"
"Oh, I sat down and helped her cry".

AUTHOR UNKNOWN

Always be there. Especially when nobody else is.

HELEN EXLEY

I have found that there is
a tremendous joy in giving.
It is a very important part
of the joy of living.

WILLIAM BLACK

A kindness given
with a smile
is like a shaft
of sunlight
on a dreary day.

PAMELA DUGDALE

Happiness is giving a little
and taking a little,
even if it is a mere dandelion.
It is worth as much as
a bouquet of red roses
wrapped in delicate lace
if it is given with care.

HELEN CADDICK, AGE 11

No one is useless in this world
who lightens the burden of it for anyone else.

CHARLES DICKENS

If I can stop one heart
from breaking,
I shall not live in vain:
If I can ease one life the aching,
Or cool one pain,
Or help one fainting robin
Unto his nest again,
I shall not live in vain.

EMILY DICKINSON

${M}$ost people don't just want soup,
they want contact
where they are appreciated,
loved, feel wanted and find some peace
in their hearts.
It's the personal touch which matters.

SISTER DOLORES

Sometimes the best
of kindnesses
is a quiet hug.

ODILE DORMEUIL

We are bound to everyone else in the world.
Whenever we help another person
we add to the common good.

MATHILDE AND SÉBASTIEN FORESTIER

Little kindnesses spread happiness.
Nothing is ever lost.

DALTON EXLEY

So many paths, that wind and wind,
While just the art of being kind
Is all the sad world needs.

ELLA WHEELER WILCOX

Throw out
the lifeline,
throw out
the lifeline,
Someone is
sinking today.

EDWARD SMITH UFFORD

Do not keep the alabaster boxes
of your love and tenderness sealed up,
until your friends are dead.
Fill their lives with sweetness.
Speak approving, cheering words
while their ears can hear them
and while their hearts can be thrilled
and made happier by them.
The kind things you mean to say
when they are gone,
say them before they go.

GEORGE W. CHILDS

The fragrance
always remains
in the hand
that gives
the rose.

HEDA BEJAR

Give help rathe

Kindness costs little
and can be practiced anywhere...
anytime...with anyone.
Kindness pauses to let another
motorist enter the freeway.
Kindness picks the last two camellias
from the bush by the front door
to give to the flowerless neighbor.

SUZANNE C. COLE

than advice.

LUC DE VAUVENARGUES

The happiness of life
is made up of minute fractions –
the little soon-forgotten
charities of a kiss,
a smile, a kind look,
a heartfelt compliment
in the disguise of a playful raillery,
and the countless other infinitesimals
of pleasant thought and feeling.

SAMUEL TAYLOR COLERIDGE

When I was going through
a very difficult time,
someone called me up
and played piano music for me
on my answering machine.
It made me feel very loved,
and I never discovered who did it.

EDITORS OF CONARI PRESS

Just a chat, a cup of tea,
a lift to the shops,
the collection of a prescription,
the caring for a cat, a listening
and a patient ear, a bunch of flowers,
a pot of jam, the first beans of the year.
A wave. A smile.
Small kindnesses, small courtesies,
small acts of friendship,
can transform the day.

DALTON EXLEY

A casual act
of kindness
can light
someone's day.

HANNAH C. KLEIN

It is one of the most beautiful compensations of this life that no one can sincerely try to help another without helping themselves.

RALPH WALDO EMERSON

Everything that is

not given is lost.

INDIAN PROVERB

The thing that lies at the foundation
of positive change,
the way I see it, is service
to a fellow human being.

LEE IACOCCA

I sit across the carriage from you on a train
bound for an unfamiliar place.
I do not know you, yet you smile at me.
Suddenly I see something familiar.
And I know that kindness travels too.

SIÂN E. MORGAN

When you show kindness to others,
they may not remember exactly
what you did or said but they will certainly
remember how you made them feel.

FROM "THE FRIENDSHIP BOOK OF FRANCIS GAY"

We have not too much time
for gladdening the hearts
of those who are travelling
the dark way with us.
Oh, be swift to love!

HENRI FRÉDÉRIC AMIEL

If you can see someone's lost,
help them out.
If it was you who was lost you'd be so glad
someone helped you.

DALTON EXLEY

...the more we truly desire to benefit others,
the greater the strength and confidence
we develop and the greater the peace
and happiness we experience.
If this still seems unlikely, it is worth asking
ourselves how else we are to do so.
With violence and aggression? Of course not.
With money? Perhaps up to a point,
but no further. But with love, by sharing
others' suffering, by recognizing ourselves
clearly in all others – especially those who
are disadvantaged and those whose rights
are not respected –
by helping them to be happy: yes.

MAHAYANA BUDDHIST QUOTATION

Give what you have
to someone, it may be better
than you dare think.

HENRY WADSWORTH LONGFELLOW

Kindness is the greatest gift
for humanity.
Nothing is more important
than to be kind to each other.

DEBASISH MRIDHA

A kind word
costs nothing
but is
beyond price.

STUART & LINDA MACFARLANE

If someone listens,
or stretches out a hand,
or whispers a kind word of encouragement,
or attempts to understand
a lonely person,
extraordinary things begin to happen.

LORETTA GIRZATIS

When you give a lifting hand
and make someone feel better for it,
you've given that person medicine.

BEAR HEART (MUSKOGEE)

Kindness eases the tension of a friend
with a shoulder and neck massage.
Kindness buys a rose from the child
selling them under the freeway
and gives it away before she arrives home.
Kindness looks at the pictures
of the new grandbaby and say,
"she's beautiful" – and means it.

SUZANNE C. COLE

It costs nothing to say a "hello"
here and there.
To friends that you pass in the street.
It costs nothing to smile at a stranger,
Or any new friend that you meet.
It costs nothing to show your emotions,
or your feelings when things don't go right.
It costs nothing to help the unfortunate,
Who are blind or who have no sight.
It costs nothing to be happy.
And happiness can be found.
Happiness is like butter,
So go on and spread some around.

JEANETTE ACHILLES, AGE 15

To be kind can be a smile, a word,
the opening of a door, an offer of assistance –
or it can be, more usefully, the scrubbing
of a floor, the cooking of a meal,
a washing load, a trunk full of shopping,
a lift to the hospital in the early hours,
a never-ending patience.

DALTON EXLEY

"Can I help?" is such a powerful phrase.
Just by asking this you can make
someone's day a lot brighter.

STUART & LINDA MACFARLANE

An unexpected
act of kindness
can be a
scintillating
rocket in a
dark sky.

CHARLOTTE GRAY

Kindness is given
so softly, so gently,
falling like tiny seeds
along our path –
and brightening it
with flowers.

ODILE DORMEUIL

You cannot do a kindness
too soon because you never know
how soon it will be too late.

RALPH WALDO EMERSON

We should give as we would receive,
cheerfully, quickly,
and without hesitation;
for there is no grace
in a benefit that sticks to the fingers.

SENECA THE YOUNGER

True Kindness is that magical something that's given for free, with no conditions and no expectations of favours in return.

SIÂN E. MORGAN

In a little Indiana town, there was
a 15-year-old boy with a brain tumor.
He was undergoing radiation and
chemotherapy treatments. As a result of those
treatments, he had lost all of his hair.
This young man's classmates spontaneously
came to the rescue... There, in the local
newspaper, was a photograph of a mother
shaving off all of her son's hair with the
family looking on approvingly.
And in the background, a group of
similarly bald young men.

HANOCH MCCARTY

So many live
on hope.
A phone call.
A knock at the door.
A letter.
Remember them.

HANNAH C. KLEIN

One word, one action, or one thought
can reduce another person's suffering
and bring him or her joy.
One word can give comfort and confidence,
destroy doubt, help someone avoid
a mistake, reconcile a conflict,
or open the door to liberation.
One action can save a person's life
or help her or him take advantage
of a rare opportunity.

THICH NHAT HANH

You never regret

A kind word
A kind gesture.
They fall like coloured pebbles into a lake,
their ripple circling out
beyond your comprehension.
You change more than you know.

PAM BROWN

Take a seed of kindness and plant it
as soon after you wake up as possible,
then keep planting them as often as you can,
all day long – and see how they grow.

SIÂN E. MORGAN

being kind.

NICOLE SHEPHERD

Always be
a little kinder
than necessary.

SIR JAMES M. BARRIE

Each and every act of kindness
done by anyone anywhere
resonates out into the world
and somehow,
mysteriously, invisibly,
and perfectly,
touches us all.

EDITORS OF CONARI PRESS

The Sufis advise us to speak
only after our words have managed
to pass through three gates.
At the first gate,
we ask ourselves,
"Are these words true?"
If so, we let them pass on;
if not, back they go.
At the second gate,
we ask, "Are they necessary?"
At the last gate we ask,
"Are they kind?"

EKNATH EASWARAN

A kind act
shines out
in a dark
world.

PAM BROWN

Tread gently
as you move
through others' lives.
Be kind.
Let them
remember you
with joy.
Never with regret.

HELEN EXLEY

The best portion of a good man's life,
His little, nameless, unremembered acts
of kindness and of love.

WILLIAM WORDSWORTH

The opportunity to practice brotherhood
presents itself every time
you meet a human being.

JANE WYMAN

A kind person
is the one who is kind to strangers.

ZAIRE BAKONGON PROVERB

A warm smile
is the
universal
language of
kindness.

WILLIAM ARTHUR WARD

Each time someone is kind,
it makes a difference to my life.
And each time that happens,
I try to do the same for someone else.
And each time that happens,
kindness spreads a little further.

SIÂN E. MORGAN

Talk to someone at the bus stop.
Carry a bag of shopping to a car.
Find space for a lost and lonely cat.
These seem like such small things.
And yet change the world a little.

DALTON EXLEY

What do we live for,
if it is not to make life less
difficult for each other?

GEORGE ELIOT (MARY ANN EVANS)

When a goose gets sick
or wounded or shot down,
two geese drop out of the formation
and follow her down
to help and protect her.
They stay with her until she is either
able to fly again or dies.
Then they start out again,
either joining another formation
or catching up with the original flock.

AUTHOR UNKNOWN

You can give without loving,
but you can never love
without giving.
The great acts of love
are done by those
who are habitually
performing small acts
of kindness.

VICTOR HUGO

You have not lived a perfect day,
even though you have
earned your money,
unless you have done something
for someone who will
never be able to repay you.

RUTH SMELTZER

Kindness trumps greed:
it asks for sharing.
Kindness trumps fear:
it calls forth gratefulness and love.
Kindness trumps even stupidity,
for with sharing and love, one learns.
It's inexpensive, simply understood,
and universally approved.

MARC ESTRIN

The only gift is a

Constant kindness
can accomplish much.
As the sun makes ice melt, kindness causes
misunderstanding, mistrust and hostility
to evaporate.

ALBERT SCHWEITZER

ortion of yourself.

RALPH WALDO EMERSON

Quiet kindnesses
repeated
a thousand
times
have the
greatest value.

HELEN EXLEY

This is what sets this tiny
opal of a planet
off from a million greater worlds
– the possibility of kindness
– the possibility of care.
Love transforms it into
a place of wonder.

PAM BROWN

When we see someone suffering,
if we touch her with compassion,
she will receive our comfort
and love, and we will also receive
comfort and love.

THICH NHAT HANH

Kindness doesn't require certificates,
courses or manuals.
Follow your heart,
Start right away,
Use it as often as you can.
That's all you'll ever need to know.

SIÂN E. MORGAN

Be patient with people.

HARRY ALTDON

Kindness is the life's blood.
Kindness makes the difference
between passion and caring.
Kindness is tenderness.
Kindness is love,
but perhaps greater than love...
Kindness is good will.
Kindness says,
"I want you to be happy."

RANDOLPH RAY

A small kindness can lighten the dreariest day.

CHARLOTTE GRAY

I expect to pass through life but once.
If therefore, there be any kindness
I can show, or any good thing I can do
to any fellow being, let me do it now,
and not defer or neglect it,
as I shall not pass this way again.

WILLIAM PENN

One good deed
spreads like a ripple
around the world.
One small kindness can touch
many people's lives.

HANNAH C. KLEIN

A kind word is lik

~ Spring day. RUSSIAN PROVERB

To be offered the unique privilege
to intervene in the life
of another human being; that to me
is the meaning of love.

ADI ROCHE

Share an umbrella
with a saturated stranger.
Give someone directions –
and walk a little way with them.
Help someone with a pushchair
on the escalator.
Kindnesses that seem insignificant.
But helping people
cope and feel supported.

DALTON EXLEY

You give but little
when you give
of your possessions.
It is when you give
of yourself
that you truly give.

KAHLIL GIBRAN

Life is so short.
Let us
make haste
to be kind.

HENRI FRÉDÉRIC AMIEL

The longer I live the more
I am convinced that the one thing
worth living for and dying for
is the privilege
of making someone more happy
and more useful.
No one who ever does anything
to help others ever makes a sacrifice.

BOOKER T. WASHINGTON

If you want to raise someone
from mud and filth,
do not think it is enough to keep standing
on top and reaching down to him
a helping hand.
You must go all the way down yourself,
down into the mud and filth.
Then take hold of him
with strong hands and pull him and yourself
out into the light.

RABBI SHELOMO

Being kind is the most important thing
I've ever been taught.
That's what my parents always told me –
more important than ambition
or success is being kind to people.
The cornerstone of my life.
What I aspire to is to be kind.

RAFE SPALL

Everyone knows of at least one
opportunity where one can help
to alleviate pain, solve a misunderstanding,
reveal the truth and make friends.

HENRY DAVID THOREAU

A look of sympathy,
of encouragement;
a hand reached out in kindness.
And all else is secondary.

HELEN EXLEY

Give a little money –
whatever is needed.
If in this hell of a world one
can bring a little joy and peace
even for a day
to a single person,
that much alone is true;
this I have learnt
after suffering all my life;
all else is mere moonshine....

SWAMI VIVEKANANDA

A random act of kindness,
no matter how small,
can make a tremendous impact
on someone else's life.

ROY T. BENNETT

A small act of kindness
may change someone's day.
A thoughtless act of unkindness
can be remembered for a lifetime.

ODILE DORMEUIL

A house where kindness lives
is a house of warmth and happiness.

HANNAH C. KLEIN

Give quickly, wildly,
a little recklessly.
Planned, controlled giving can add
a coldness, a distance.
"Go for it," in all things in life –
especially when you feel
kindness coming on!

HELEN EXLEY

The greatest charity is to enable the poor to earn a living.

THE TALMUD

Wise sayings often fall on barren ground,
but a kind word is never thrown away.

SIR ARTHUR HELPS

When I was young,
I admired clever people.
Now that I am old,
I admire kind people.

ABRAHAM HESCHEL

If you can only do something small, do it.
It may well be the vital stitch
that makes someone's life perfect.

CHARLOTTE GRAY

There are in every street,
small pools of kindliness.
In every city,
in every village.
It takes one wise and courageous
person to link them.

ODILE DORMEUIL

Whatever the reason, never say
"I'm too busy" – never even think that.
Always say instead
"Yes, I will see what I can do."

HELEN EXLEY

In one life we touch a thousand lives.

You are more than you believe.

You can make changes.

By good work.

By thought.

By words.

By kindness.

Changes that help the world to grow.

PAM BROWN

Kind words
can be short
and easy to speak,
but their echoes
are endless.

MOTHER TERESA

Give up your seat
for someone who
needs it more
than you do on
the bus or train.
Always.

DALTON EXLEY

Do anything, but

Someday you will say something.

Or reach out a hand.

And you will change a life forever.

And walk away,

not knowing.

Be kind

– kindness works miracles.

ODILE DORMEUIL

et it produce joy.

WALT WHITMAN

It is a terrible thing,
this kindness that human beings
do not lose.
Terrible because when we are finally
naked in the dark and cold,
it is all we have.
We who are so rich,
so full of strength,
wind up with that small change.
We have nothing else to give.

URSULA K. LE GUIN

All the beautiful sentiments in the world weigh less than a single lovely action.

JAMES RUSSELL LOWELL

Thank you to all the people in the world
who are always ten per cent kinder
than they need to be.
That's what really makes the world go round.

HELEN EXLEY

Be especially kind to those
who are least likely to return it.

STUART & LINDA MACFARLANE

Giving is so often thought
of in terms of the things we give,
but our greatest giving is of our time,
and kindness, and even comfort
for those who need it.

JOYCE SEQUICHE HIFLER

Be kind whenever possible. It is always possible.

THE DALAI LAMA

Let us be kinder
to one another.

ALDOUS HUXLEY'S LAST WORDS

One kind word
can warm
three winter months.

JAPANESE PROVERB

Never, if possible, lie down at night
without being able to say:
"I have made one human being
at least a little wiser,
or a little happier,
or a little better this day."

CHARLES KINGSLEY